D0778629

Spy
Files

CODES and CIPHERS

Adrian Gilbert

QEB Publishing

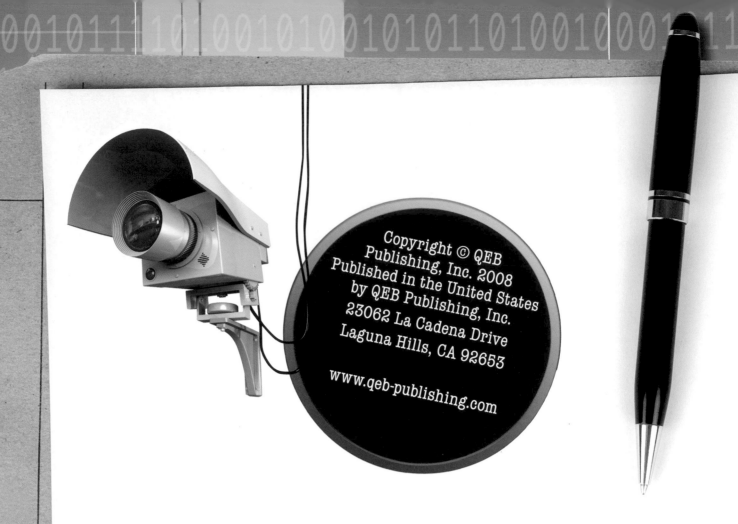

Copyright © QEB
Publishing, Inc. 2008
Published in the United States
by QEB Publishing, Inc.
23062 La Cadena Drive
Laguna Hills, CA 92653

www.qeb-publishing.com

Library of Congress Control Number: 2008010029

ISBN 978 1 59566 594 2

Printed and bound in the United States

Author Adrian Gilbert
Consultant Clive Gifford
Editor Amanda Askew
Designer Lisa Peacock
Picture Researcher Maria Joannou

Publisher Steve Evans
Creative Director Zeta Davies

Picture credits (t=top, b=bottom, l=left, r=right)
Alamy Images Mary Evans Picture Library 6b,
Pictorial Press Ltd 23t, Visual Arts Library (London) 7
Corbis 15b, 20t, Bettmann 5b, 6t, 12b, 14, 17,
19, 24, 25t, Hulton-Deutsch Collection 16, Jeffrey L
Rotman 28b, Reuters 15t
DK Images Andy Crawford 13
Getty Images David Savill/Topical Press Agency/
Hulton Archive 8b, Hulton Archive 8t, 10t, 21,
Popperfoto 10b, 26t, 27t, Time & Life Pictures 12t
Istockphoto 25b
Photoshot 5t, UPPA 9, World Illustrated 18t
Rex Features 18b, 20b, Everett 27b, Greg
Mathieson 26b, Lewis Durham 29t
Science Photo Library James King-Holmes/
Bletchley Park Trust 23b, Michael Donne 11
The International Spy Museum 28t, 29b
Topham Picturepoint The National Archives/
HIP 22

Words in **bold** can be found in the
glossary on page 30.

Contents

Codes and ciphers

Codes and ciphers are ways of scrambling up words to make them **impossible to understand**.

The only people who can work out the code are the person sending the message and the person receiving it.

Codes and ciphers

88   *   7-2

CODES

Codes involve the replacement of a whole word by letters, numbers or symbols, so the word "missile" might be **8675**, or the symbol ✦. Both the sender and receiver of the message must work with the same **codebook**.

CODE WORDS

To jumble up a message is called **encoding** or **enciphering**, while to change the message back to the original is called **decoding** or **deciphering**. **Cryptology** is the study of codes and ciphers.

RADIO CODES

Codes and ciphers were first used by the ancient Egyptians, but were not written down properly until the 16th century. The introduction of **radio communications** in the early 1900s changed the world of cryptology forever.

▲ A German field radio from World War I (1914–1918), when radio communication was just beginning.

▲ A German telephone unit at work. Even telephone conversations could be listened in to with the right equipment.

RADIO MESSAGES

Using radios, messages were **broadcast** over vast distances, but the messages could be heard by anyone listening in with a radio receiver. To stop the enemy being able to understand the messages, complex codes and ciphers were developed.

CIPHERS

Ciphers are the replacement of a single letter by another letter or number. Ciphers are more flexible than codes, but are usually easier to break.

Codes and ciphers 49?ir p3? 4xc-i&r

The Caesar cipher

The Roman soldier and statesman Julius Caesar developed a cipher system to send letters back to Rome when he was away fighting.

It used two alphabets—one above the other but with one alphabet moved a few letters along, maybe two or more.

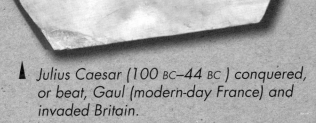

▲ *Julius Caesar (100 BC–44 BC) conquered, or beat, Gaul (modern-day France) and invaded Britain.*

▲ Johannes Trithemius significantly developed the science of cryptology.

The Caesar cipher was greatly improved by a German abbot called Johannes Trithemius, whose cipher table was used by spies in the 16th century. In 1518, he published *Polygraphia*, the first printed book on cryptology.

6

MAKE YOUR OWN CAESAR CIPHER

Copy out the alphabets below—notice that the bottom alphabet has been shifted two letters to the right.

A B C D E F G H I J K L M N O P Q R S T U V W X Y Z

C D E F G H I J K L M N O P Q R S T U V W X Y Z A B

To encipher a message, replace each letter on the top row with the one directly below it. The message

THREE ENEMY MISSILES FIRED

will now read

VJTGG GPGOA OKUUKGU HKTGF

It is complete nonsense to anyone, except you!

Caesar accepts the surrender of the Gaulish leader, Vercingetorix. News of this victory would have been sent to Rome in code.

Code breaking

As soon as a code has been invented, people will try to break it.

Simple ciphers are easy to break because patterns can be seen in the message. The most common letter in the English language is **E**, followed by **T, N, O, R, I, A**, and **S**. It is also helpful to know that **T** is the most common first letter of a word and **E** is the most common last letter.

► *The Room 40 code-breakers helped in the war against German U-boats—a major threat to British shipping.*

BREAKING A CAESAR CIPHER

Although easy to use, the Caesar cipher is also easy to break. Knowing that **E** is the most common letter, it is always worth looking for it in an enciphered message.

In the enciphered message,

VJTGG GPGOA OKUUKGU HKTGF

there are six **G**s, by far the most common letter in this message. As **E** is two letters back in the alphabet from **G** we could try moving all the letters in the message back two letters. If we do, then we will find the original message—three enemy missiles fired.

Admiral Sir Reginald Hall (second from right), was one of the chiefs of Room 40.

ROOM 40

During World War I (1914–1918), British Navy code-breakers—known as Room 40—pioneered, or significantly developed, the science of modern code breaking. They were able to read large amounts of German coded messages.

ZIMMERMANN TELEGRAM

One of Room 40's success stories was reading the Zimmermann **telegram** in April 1917. German foreign minister Arthur Zimmermann sent it to the Mexican **government**. The Germans promised to give American territory to Mexico if Mexico attacked the USA. Knowledge of the telegram helped push the United States toward war with Germany.

British Prime Minister David Lloyd George (left) made sure the Zimmermann telegram was shown to the Americans.

Morse Code

During the 1840s, U.S. inventor Samuel Morse developed a code.

It could be sent electronically along telegraph wires as a series of short and long pulses. The pulses were written out as short dots and long dashes.

▼ British soldiers undergo training in electrical equipment during World War II (1939–1945).

▲ American inventor Samuel Morse (1791–1872) developed a very effective electrical code.

RADIO TRANSMISSION

Although it was made for ordinary types of communication, Morse Code has been used by secret agents for long-distance radio communication. During radio **transmissions**, Morse is clearer and easier to hear than the spoken voice. A spy would code his message before sending it by Morse.

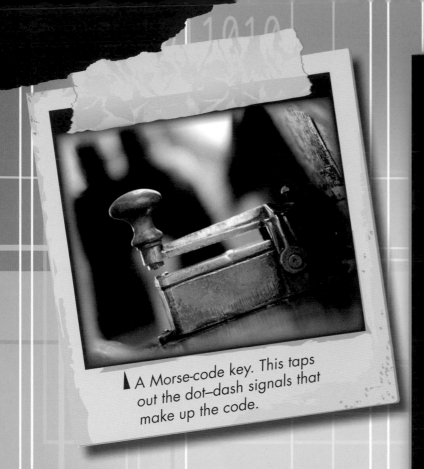

A Morse-code key. This taps out the dot–dash signals that make up the code.

International Morse Code

A	•—	S	•••
B	—•••	T	—
C	—•—•	U	••—
D	—••	V	•••—
E	•	W	•——
F	••—•	X	—••—
G	——•	Y	—•——
H	••••	Z	——••
I	••	0	—————
J	•———	1	•————
K	—•—	2	••———
L	•—••	3	•••——
M	——	4	••••—
N	—•	5	•••••
O	———	6	—••••
P	•——•	7	——•••
Q	——•—	8	———••
R	•—•	9	————•

EVERYDAY SITUATIONS

As secret agents and people in the armed forces are taught Morse Code, they are able to communicate with each other when they are in danger. They can flash warnings to each other at night using a torch, or when held in a prison they have been able to tap messages using radiators and water pipes.

SECRET BLINKING

American naval pilot Jeremiah Denton was shot down over North Vietnam in 1965, and he was forced to give a television interview. During the interview, Denton secretly blinked his eyes in Morse Code to spell out the word "TORTURE." This told U.S. **intelligence** that his captors were **torturing** him and his fellow **POWs**.

11

Visual codes

Spies also communicate through visual codes, **especially when they are meeting each other.**

The meeting of two spies in a **hostile country** can be dangerous, so they are trained to spot visual signals. If a spy knows they are being followed by an enemy agent, they will warn the spy they are meeting by making an agreed signal, such as wearing a coat in a certain way.

▲ Two spies meet in Berlin. They may use visual codes, such as the color of their coats, to identify each other.

▲ In his many books, Baden-Powell gave useful hints to spies on using visual codes.

LORD ROBERT BADEN-POWELL

The founder of the **Scouting movement**, Baden-Powell (1857–1941) trained as a scout in the British Army. He used this knowledge to carry out spying operations in foreign countries. He described how he took on the disguise of an innocent butterfly collector while sketching details of a fortress in the **Balkans**.

HIDDEN MESSAGES

Secret information may be hidden in ordinary drawings or pictures. Newspapers are also used to convey hidden messages. A seemingly ordinary advert may tell a spy that he must arrange a meeting with his **handler**.

HIDDEN FORTS

Baden-Powell drew innocent-looking sketches of a butterfly and a leaf while on a trip to the Balkans, where he pretended to be a butterfly collector. However, the drawings are not what they seem. They actually provide details of enemy forts. Baden-Powell was so confident of visual code that he showed them to government officials to admire his artistic skills!

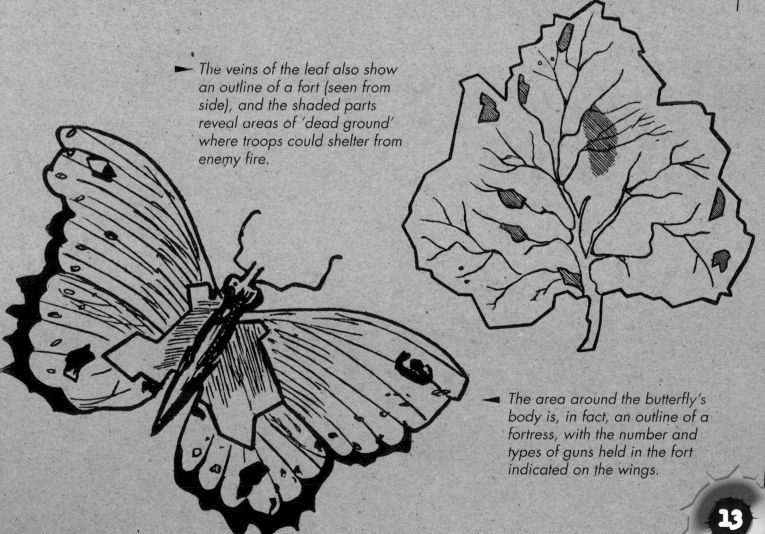

► The veins of the leaf also show an outline of a fort (seen from side), and the shaded parts reveal areas of 'dead ground' where troops could shelter from enemy fire.

◄ The area around the butterfly's body is, in fact, an outline of a fortress, with the number and types of guns held in the fort indicated on the wings.

Navajo code talkers

A Native American speaks down his radio, sure in the knowledge that he cannot be understood by the enemy.

During World War II (1939–1945), Philip Johnston came up with the idea of using the language of the Native-American Navajo **tribe to prevent the Japanese from listening in to U.S. radio conversations.**

Johnston, a non-native speaker of the language, persuaded the U.S. Marines to use the Navajo code. Navajo is an extremely complex, unwritten language without an alphabet or other symbols. Johnston estimated that only 30 non-Navajos knew the language and none of them were Japanese.

NEW MILITARY TERMS

The Navajo language did not have names for many of the U.S. military terms, and so the code-talkers worked out their own.

Iron-fish = submarine
Whale = battleship
Hummingbird = fighter aircraft
Eggs = bombs

FAST CODES

The main job of the code talkers was to broadcast orders and other battlefield information over radios and telephones. The code talkers took just 20 seconds to code and send a short message. It would have taken a normal coding machine 30 minutes to do the same job. The Japanese were completely bewildered by the code talkers and never managed to break the code.

▲ President George W Bush awards Navajo code talker Chester Nez the Congressional Gold Medal to honor his war service.

Top Secret!

British officers communicated with each other in Latin during the Second Boer War (1899–1902) because Latin was unknown to ordinary Boer farmers.

➤ A code-talking team send orders to a U.S. Marine unit in the war against the Japanese in the Pacific Ocean.

One-time pads

One-time pads are one of the most secure types of code.

They consist of two separate pads, or small books, of **randomly generated** letters or numbers arranged in small groups. Each group stands for a word or phrase.

► *One-time pads were very small, making them easy to hide.*

The sender has one book, and the receiver has the other. Every time a page of the pad is used it is destroyed—it really is a one-time pad. What makes the system so secure is that it is used only once. No pattern of coded letters is allowed to develop. However, to be totally secure, the letter groups must be random and the pad used once.

The system was developed by Americans, Gilbert Vernam and Captain Joseph Mauborgne, in 1918. The system was popular and intelligence agencies used it around the world during World War II and into the Cold War.

Top Secret!

Soviet intelligence often gave its spies one-time pads printed on tiny sheets of "flash paper" that burnt immediately if lit and left no ash.

16

MAKE YOUR OWN ONE-TIME PAD

Choose a group of random numbers, such as
6523 1427 2187 3624 1321 7342 1165 4129
These are your pad numbers, which you and the other spy would have.

Next you're going to create your message. Write out the alphabet from A to Z.
Then write out 01 to 26 next to it.

A 01	D 04	G 07	J 10	M 13	P 16	S 19	V 22	Y 25
B 02	E 05	H 08	K 11	N 14	Q 17	T 20	W 23	Z 26
C 03	F 06	I 09	L 12	O 15	R 18	U 21	X 24	

To create a message, replace each letter with its number. The message **I HAVE MADE A CODE** will now read **09080122051301040501 03150405**

Then split the long number into groups of four—**0908 0122 0513 0104 0501 0315 0405**

Now to encipher the message! You must add four 0s to the beginning of the message numbers.

Pad numbers   **6523 1427 2187 3624 1321 7342 1165 4129**

Message numbers **0000 0908 0122 0513 0104 0501 0315 0405**

To make your final code, add the top and bottom numbers together.
So 6523+0000=6523, 1427+0908=2335, 2187+0122=2309, and so on.

The final numbers make your one-time pad code!

6523 2335 2309 4137 1425 7842 1480 4534

It's easy for your friend to decipher the message if they have the pad numbers.

Pad numbers   **6523 1427 2187 3624 1321 7342 1165 4129**

One-time pad code **6523 2335 2309 4137 1425 7842 1480 4534**

To decode the message, take away the pad numbers from the one-time pad code, for example, 2334-1427=0908, 2309-2187=0122

According to the alphabet numbers, the first two letters are IH and the second two letters are AV. See, your code works!

17

Cipher machines

Cipher discs and then cipher rotors were developed to speed up the process of enciphering messages.

The first-known cipher disc was developed by Leon Baptista Alberti in the 15th century. These simple cipher discs were easy to decipher. From about 1900 onward, they were replaced by **rotor systems** that used **polyalphabetic substitution**.

▲ The Italian cryptographer Alberti constructed the first-known cipher disc during the 15th century.

In this system, each letter would be substituted by a different letter every time. For example, the two letter **E**s in the word "three" would be enciphered to show different letters, such as **Y** and **G**.

◄ An electronic cipher machine from World War II, which used a series of rotors to encipher the message.

ELECTRIC CIPHER MACHINES

The polyalphabetic system was made practical by the development of electric cipher machines, invented by the American Edward Hebern and the Swede Boris Hagelin. Their ciphers were very hard to break, but quick and easy to use.

▲ Swedish cryptographer Boris Hagelin developed cipher machines for the French secret service and US Army.

MAKE YOUR OWN CIPHER DISC

Cut out two cardboard discs. One should be 8 inches in **diameter** and the other should be 10 inches in diameter. Pin the two discs together. Carefully write out two alphabets around the edge of each disc, so that they line up together. To send a ciphered message, the sender and the receiver must agree on how many letters the inner disc is moved around. If they agreed on four letters, **E** on the inner disc would line up with **A** on the outer disc. To make the cipher harder to break, the number of letters the inner disc is moved along can be constantly changed.

▲ A simple cipher disc.

Purple intelligence

In 1938, the Japanese introduced a new, high-level cipher machine, which was called Purple in the United States.

Led by famous cryptographer William Friedman, an American team immediately set about trying to break its ciphers. Friedman's team had already broken an earlier, similar cipher called Red, and they used that knowledge to build a **replica** of the Purple machine.

▲ William Friedman explains how his highly successful deciphering machine works.

"PURPLE"

THIS IS THE LARGEST OF THREE SURVIVING PIECES OF THE FAMOUS JAPANESE DIPLOMATIC CIPHER MACHINE. IT WAS RECOVERED FROM THE WRECKAGE OF THE JAPANESE EMBASSY IN BERLIN, 1945.

PURPLE

BREAKING THE CIPHER

The Japanese did not use rotors in their machines. Instead, they used a type of switch found in telephone exchanges. The Americans realized this and were able to build a replica machine and break the Japanese cipher.

◄ **Stepping switches** of the type used by the Japanese in their Purple cipher machine.

AMERICAN SUCCESS

Due to the intelligence gained from Purple, the United States had a good idea of Japanese **military** intentions throughout the war. Intelligence of Japanese ship movements was vital to American success at the Battle of Midway in June 1942, one of the crucial battles of World War II.

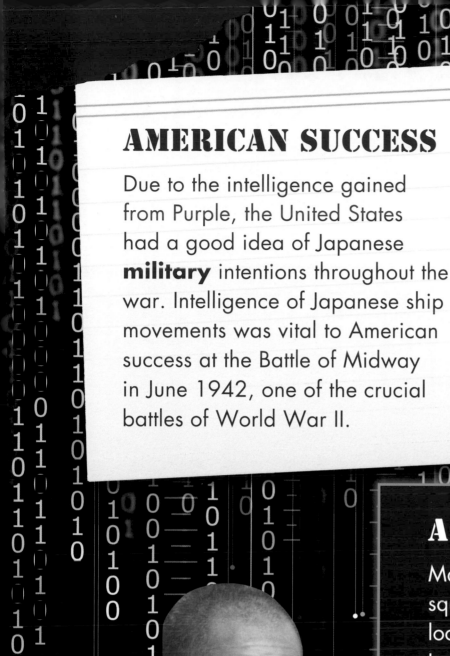

Top Secret!
William Friedman called his team of cryptologists "magicians" and the decrypted intelligence was then termed "Magic."

A BIT OF MAGIC

Magic intelligence enabled a squadron of U.S. fighter planes to locate and shoot down Admiral Isoroku Yamamoto. He was flying to inspect Japanese troops on the Solomon Islands in April 1943.

◄ Admiral Yamamoto was the most famous victim of American code-breaking intelligence during World War II.

Enigma

During the 1930s, the Germans introduced a cipher machine called Enigma.

They used Enigma throughout World War II and believed it to be unbreakable. However, work on breaking Enigma had begun in Poland before the beginning of the war, and then in France and Britain.

▼ *Colossus was built at Bletchley Park, London, England. It played a key role in breaking the German Enigma codes.*

COMPLEX MACHINE

Enigma was a very complex machine that the Germans used to make decoding more difficult. Mathematician Alan Turing built an early form of electronic computer—called Colossus—to help break the German ciphers.

ULTRA

The code name for the intelligence that came from Enigma was Ultra. This information played a major part in the **Allied** victory over Germany in World War II.

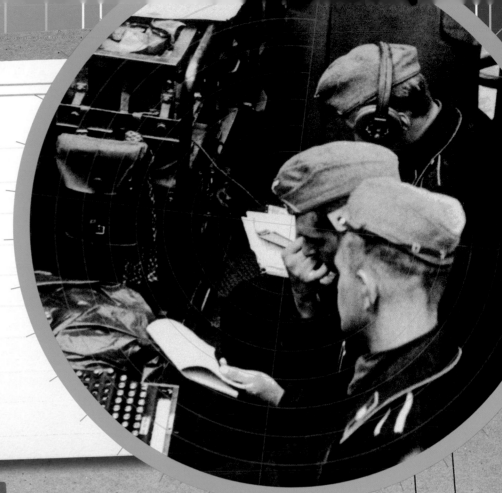

▶ *Signalers from a German tank unit prepare to send an Enigma message from the battlefield.*

BLETCHLEY PARK

Bletchley Park was an old country house north of London, England, that became the headquarters for code breakers. At one point, 9,000 people were working at Bletchley Park—many of them were excellent at problem solving. As well as code-breakers, mathematicians, and language experts, the workers included chess champions and top crossword puzzle solvers.

◀ *An example of a German Enigma machine, with the series of rotors in place (beyond the keyboard).*

23

Secret writing

Codes and ciphers jumble up the meaning of a message, but secret writing completely hides the message, so only the receiver knows it has been sent.

The oldest form of secret writing —the wet system—uses invisible inks, which can be created using everyday sources such as fruit juices, milk, and even urine.

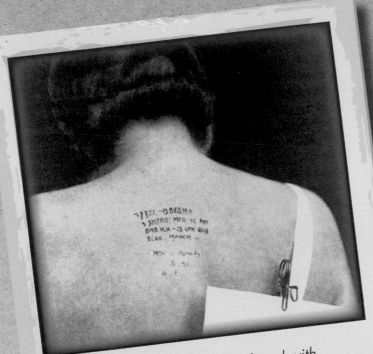

▶ A female Belgian spy was found with a message written on her back in invisible ink.

TRANSFER SYSTEMS

The transfer system is more complicated. The sender writes a message onto paper that has been treated with chemicals. The paper stays blank after the message is written. The receiver then transfers, or rubs, the paper onto another piece of paper and the message is revealed.

INVISIBLE MESSAGE

Spies usually write their secret message in between the lines of another piece of ordinary writing. This will help to disguise the reason for the secret message—sending a blank piece of paper might look suspicious.

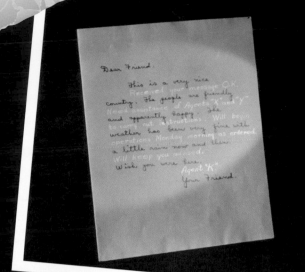

▲ An **ultra-violet** light reveals a secret message hidden within an ordinary letter.

WRITE YOUR OWN SECRET MESSAGE

Using a thin wax candle as your pen, write a message on a piece of blank paper. Then tell your friend to use a crayon of any color and rub it over your message. Your secret message will begin to appear because the crayon will not mark the paper where the wax sits!

SECRET

Microdots

From the 1860s onward, photographic film was reduced in size to carry messages in as small a way as possible.

The Germans developed very small messages called **microdots** in the years before World War II. They were soon followed by the Soviet Union.

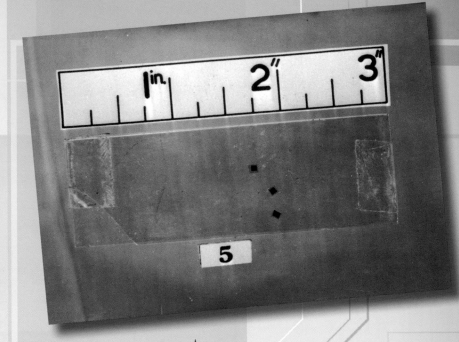

▲ The tiny size of these three microdots can be seen when put beside an inch-rule.

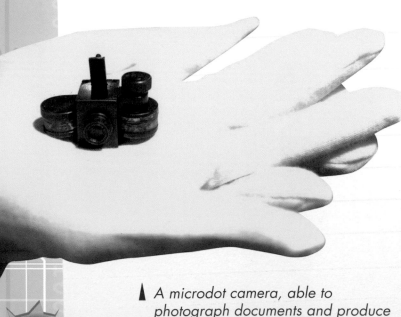

▲ A microdot camera, able to photograph documents and produce microdots less than 0.03 inches in diameter.

MICRODOT VIEWER

Microdots are images of documents, drawings, or photographs that are shrunk down to tiny sizes. A typical microdot will be only 0.03 inches in diameter, and some are even smaller. They can only be read using a microscope or special microdot viewer.

HIDING THE DOTS

Microdots can be hidden in hollowed-out rings or coins, stuck on letters, or hidden in clothing. Soviet spies used to make a small slit with a razor in the edge of a postcard, slip in the microdot with a pair of tweezers, and seal up the slit with flour and water paste.

> ▼ Part of the Russian text of a microdot document taken from Soviet spy Helen Kroger.

▲ A scene from the film Mission Impossible 3, which features microdots and other tricks and tools from the world of spying.

Top Secret!

Spies in the American Civil War (1861–1865) hid tiny messages in hollow metal buttons on their clothing. They hoped that if they were searched, the messages would not be found.

MICRODOTS AT THE MOVIES

In the film *Mission Impossible 3*, a microdot is hidden on the back of a postage stamp and contains a magnetically stored video file. Microdots also feature in James Bond films, such as *You Only Live Twice*.

Radio communications

Radio receivers and transmitters are essential tools of the secret agent, to receive and send information without delay.

Messages are encoded or enciphered before being sent. To avoid **Radio Detection Finders** (RDF), messages are sent as **burst transmissions**, so the pre-recorded message is made smaller and broadcasting time is reduced.

◄ A listening device produced by the **CIA,** camouflaged to look like a tree stump.

HIDDEN RADIOS

Until fairly recently, radios were big and bulky and **concealment** was a problem. However, since the widespread use of **transistors** in the 1960s and **silicon chips** in the 1990s, radios have become much smaller.

▲ This tiny radio transmitter in a tie shows how new technology has made concealment easy.

SUITCASE RADIOS

World War II radios were large and heavy. One attempt to conceal them was by hiding them in suitcases. Suitcase radios were used by all sides during the war.

▲ A suitcase radio was often used in World War II.

As well as building suitcase radios, **SOE** officer John Brown designed a biscuit-tin radio, in which the separate bits of the radio could be packed away into biscuit-tins and then be reassembled for making broadcasts. As radios became smaller after World War II, they were hidden in briefcases, and then lunch boxes.

Top Secret!

To make sure that a spy's suitcase radio did not look out of place in Occupied Europe, OSS obtained suitcases from European refugees who had fled to America.

◄ A **KGB** radio transmitter from the 1960s, hidden in the heel of the shoe.

RADIO TRAFFIC

Radios transmissions are easy to listen in to, however. During the Cold War, American spy satellites were able to "overhear" the conversations of top Soviet leaders, talking to each other through radios in their cars.

GLOSSARY

Allies/Allied The World War II alliance between Britain, the Soviet Union, and the USA (and other, smaller countries) against Germany, Japan and Italy.

Balkans The area of south-eastern Europe containing the countries of Greece, Bulgaria, Albania, and much of the former Yugoslavia.

Broadcast To send out by radio or television signals.

Burst transmissions A radio message sent by a spy that is pre-recorded and then electronically compressed. This ensures that the time spent sending the message is very short, and so is difficult for anyone else to detect.

CIA Central Intelligence Agency, the intelligence-collecting organization of the USA.

Codebook A specially produced book that has details of codes or ciphers for the sending of secret messages. Both the sender and receiver need to work with the same codebook.

Concealment Hiding something carefully.

Cryptology The study of codes and ciphers.

Decipher To convert an enciphered message back into its original form, so that it can be understood.

Decode To convert an encoded message back into its original form, so that it can be understood.

Diameter The length of a straight line passing through the centre of a circle.

Encipher To convert a message into a cipher.

Encode To convert a message into a code.

Government A group of people who rule a country or state.

Hostile country A country belonging to the enemy.

Handler Another word for a controller—an agent who directs and supports spies working undercover.

Intelligence Organization that seeks secret information.

KGB The combined security and intelligence services of the Soviet Union.

Latin The language of ancient Rome, but widely studied in Western schools until the 20th century. It was occasionally used as a secret language.

Microdot A photograph, especially of a document, reduced to a very small size.

Military Relating to the army, navy or airforce.

Navajo A Native American of New Mexico and Arizona, USA.

Occupied Europe Those countries in Europe under German control during World War II.

OSS Office of Strategic Studies, an intelligence and special operations organization formed by the USA during World War II.

Polyalphabetic substitution An enciphering system in which a letter is substituted by a different letter every time it is used. This makes ciphers much harder to break. The German Enigma machine used this system at a very high level of complexity.

POW Prisoner of war.

Radio communication A system for transmitting signals through space, using a transmitter and a receiver. Widely used by spies for sending messages over long distances.

Radio Direction Finders A device able to locate radio signals and the geographical position of the radio transmitter.

Randomly generated An electronic method of finding random numbers —numbers that have no relation to each other.

Refugee Someone who has been forced to flee their country or home.

Replica An exact copy of something.

Rotor system The series of rotor wheels or cylinders used to make polyalphabetic substitutions.

Scouting movement The international youth organization founded by Robert Baden-Powell.

Silicon chip A very small device that uses a crystal of a material called silicon, and is used to carry out key electronic functions at great speed.

SOE Special Operations Executive, an undercover special operations and sabotage organization set up by Britain to attack the Germans in Occupied Europe.

Soviet Relating to a country in Europe and Asia, between 1917 and 1991.

Stepping switch A device that allows an electrical signal to be connected to one of many other connections.

Telegram A message sent by telegraph.

Torture To cause serious pain as a punishment or to make someone do something.

Transistor A small piece of electronic equipment in radios and televisions that controls the flow of electricity.

Transmission The sending of a signal or message by electrical means.

Ultra-violet A form of light that cannot normally be seen with the naked eye.

Visual code Any type of code that does not use words to get its message across.

INDEX